THE DREAMS BENEATH DESIGN

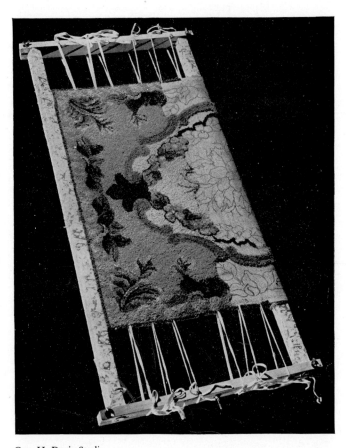

Geo. H. Davis Studio

A Hooked Rug in the Making

THE DREAMS
BENEATH DESIGN

A Story of the History and Background of the
Designs of Hooked Rugs

By

PEARL K. McGOWN

PUBLISHED BY

PEARL K. McGOWN

TO MY MOTHER

Who dreams shall live! And if we do not dream
Then we shall build no Temple into Time . . .
. . . Say nevermore
That dreams are fragile things. What else endures
Of all this broken world save only dreams!

—Dana Burnet

CONTENTS

The illustrations in this book are only a few of the several hundred patterns known to hookers as HooKraft Designs and Pearl Patterns, which Mrs. McGown has either reproduced or originated. Her studio is in her home in West Boylston, Mass., where she welcomes all who are interested in this craft.

LIST OF ILLUSTRATIONS

PART I

A Century Ago

*Y*OU who never hooked a rug may not understand, —but you who have, will know and acknowledge the fascination of this old handicraft. But whether you have or not, you may be interested in the history and the background of the designs of these heirlooms which are so treasured to-day. They are choice bits of evidence of creative artistry from the past century and a half.

You who have little imagination may be unable to project yourself into the daily life of a century ago. But you who have imagination—and how much fuller life can be with it—will enjoy deserting to-day's intricate and complex life, and go back with me in fancy to the beginning of the nineteenth century.

What was life like in 1800? Have you ever stopped to think?

You are living to-day in a period when thermostat control provides an even temperature within your home regardless of the seasons. Electricity carries perfect lighting facilities to every corner of your rooms, operates your radio which brings the whole world to your ears, cooks your food, and performs almost every hand or foot power from shaving to running your sewing machine.

To-day a wireless message from Boston to London will be received within ten minutes, in some cases much less. By telephone you may converse with one across the continent as quickly as with one across the street. Photo-radio will transmit your likeness from one continent to the other within five minutes. Your automobile will carry you over smoothly paved highways into the very heart of most of the mountainous regions of America. Luxurious liners, with every conceivable modern convenience, will cross the

Atlantic Ocean in less than four days, or you may race from New York across the continent in fifty-seven hours on the new stream-lined trains. But if speed is what you demand, try flying from the Atlantic to the Pacific Ocean in a day!

Yet, if you take this imaginary trip with me, you must first wipe out every one of the inventions which have made these miracles possible, and many more along with them, to project yourself into the period which began with the year 1800.

How did people live then? Farmers generally were still producing everything necessary for the use of their household, including their clothing. Clothing! Think what that one word meant in 1800. From the wool that had been grown on the backs of the sheep and carded on the home farm, yarn was spun and dyed with dyes that came from the barks, roots, blossoms, and leaves of Mother Nature, and woven into cloth on the loom that may, or may not, have been made on the farm too. Those were days in which things were made to last and live!

Fireplaces must be kept brightly burning, and even then you warmed one side at a time. But before even this comfort was possible, the logs must first be cut, hauled, sawed, and split, and were usually secured from your own woodlands.

Light came from softly glowing candles, used sparingly, for they required much saving of grease and hours of labor. Food was cooked before the embers of the open fireplaces or in the brick ovens, and most of the ingredients or materials were first raised upon your own farm. For these were days of farms,—these were days when there were no thickly settled manufacturing towns or centers. There were no manufacturing mills and few shops. You shaved yourself, honed your own razor, and sewed by hand for even the sewing machine had not then been conceived.

Messages could only be sent by person, and the fastest means was by horseback. You could only converse with those within the sound of your voice. Photographs were not known, and if you wished to produce a likeness of a loved one, it was done by oils or water colors in the hands of an artist.

The heart of the mountainous regions was known only by the Indians. Sixty miles a day was considered a long trip in any horse-drawn vehicle. Sailing ships were the means of crossing oceans and the length of the trip across the Atlantic could not be foretold. It might be anywhere from two to six months.

To cross our continent you usually travelled in a covered wagon drawn by a yoke of oxen, and were accompanied by several other stouthearted pioneers, all prepared to open fire upon the Indians in order to reach your destination safely.

The birds reigned supremely in the air.

At the beginning of this marvellous century, Thomas Jefferson was President, Alexander Hamilton had not yet fought his fatal duel, and Daniel Webster was just a graduate from Dartmouth College, where he had already become known as a promising young orator. Across the ocean the great Emperor Napoleon was nearing the height of his career.

During the next fifty years, great changes were made in the history of the greater nations, many of the primitive ways of living were changed by science and invention, and our own country went through one war and was on the threshold of another.

Now it was in this period from 1800 to about 1850 that most of the rugs which I am going to term "originals" were designed and made. My story will not deal with the technique of hooking, or the vast amount which can be written in regard to making these hooked rugs, but rather with the dreams beneath the designs, and their history.

So these original rugs are anywhere from seventy to a a hundred and thirty-five years old, or an average of a century.

A century! Did you ever look about you at the familiar and beloved objects in your home, and wonder how many of them would resist the vicissitudes of time? Or even a century?

Let us project ourselves, for a moment, into the year 2038. Who will have this comfortable old rocker? Where will that lovely old mahogany table be? Will these pictures that I have loved so well be discarded? My piano will be gone. I see the radio disappearing in just a few months. My davenport within a half a century will be re-covered many times over. What will be left? Can I really hope that anything here will then be in existence?

In the meantime, if it does exist, it will have to endure the possibility of fire, water, floods, wear, and worst of all, the carelessness and indifference of the intervening generations, who may not have the proper perspective to appreciate them.

Since you can face the truth and see the possibility of most of these beloved furnishings, which are filled with sentiment, swept away with the coming generations, then would it not be interesting if we could really know which of these things, if any, will be in existence in 2038? Not only in existence, but perhaps prized, sought, and valued at fabulous prices, simply because of their origin, their evidence of a clever art, handicraft or even a period of time. Or perhaps, as I view these old designs of hooked rugs now, as a story of one woman, evidence of her characteristics, a tale which tells of her industry, her cleverness, art, patience, perseverance, and ambition.

Whatever it may be, it will no doubt be the things

which you least expected. It may be something which even your own family condescendingly tolerates, or perhaps even scorns.

We are all here!
Father, mother, sister, brothers,
All who hold each other dear,
Each chair is filled—we're all at home . . .
It is not often thus around
Our old familiar hearth we're found,
Bless, then, the meeting and the spot . . .
CHARLES SPRAGUE

My conscience never gives me any peace as I recall the queer, crude hooked rugs which my mother designed and hooked within our family circle. She called it her "recreation." She always managed, in spite of the fact that she bore and reared eleven children, to find time to do two average sized rugs during each winter. And they had to be made in the evenings, when the housework was finally done.

Then the family gathered around the center table to read or work. Then Dad smoked the room blue with his favorite pipe, and I sat beneath the frame stretched over the corners of four chairs, feeding the rags to Mother as she worked. I can remember well hearing her plan the design as she hooked. "I think I'll hook a flower in this corner, and put a row of red around the edge." (She loved red, and I inherited her passion for it.) The rags were cut wide and clipped and the pile was high. The colors were gay, and the rug when finished was something made out of just what she happened to have, but it served many, many years of usefulness.

As I grew older, especially when I had my Saturday chores to do, these rugs were just something which had to be shaken and swept on the day which I thought had been made for play. I did a thoroughly good job, therefore, at shaking, for I always hoped if I shook long and hard enough that some day they would wear out and we could then have "store" rugs like those of our neighbors. Ah, me! What would I give to have those same rugs today. The home was eventually broken up—the fate of all homes, no matter how many years it may be delayed—, and the rugs disappeared in the auction. Who knows where they are to-day? I'd give a plenty to find them, those rugs which my mother made in those long winter evenings. Those evenings were in a period when there were few outside interests to take us away from home. I can recall the contentment in the faces about me—Dad, puffing as he smoked, occasionally reading aloud to Mother some news of interest, the boys with their books, the girls with their mending or sewing, and Mother, happily hooking at her rug.

Well, that was only a little more than a third of a century, yet here I am wishing for those rugs which several years ago disappeared into the nowhere. A century is *such* a long time!

Long years he labored
Faithfully with hands and mind
And never shirked.
In service he could find
Contentment; and he
Of his handiwork was proud,
As a master craftsman
Had a right to be.
As a skilled artisan
He found no greater bliss
Than fashioning
Things beautiful, like this.

ARTHUR E. WINCHESTER

But to go back a century! Those were days when every hour held its duty. Diaries of that period exist to tell of the tasks of each day and in their details record the diligence with which they were carried out. Hooking was treated more as a pastime than a duty. This was a pleasure to be indulged in only as they had finished their household tasks, their carding, spinning and weaving of wearing apparel. Then only could their time be spent in hooking, even though the product was to be used for the comfort and adornment of the home. How they must have hurried through some of these tasks, to gain an extra hour or two on their rugs. (We know, don't we?)

The earliest hookers must have been creative, for they had to produce their own designs. Here was an opportunity to combine many arts in one, the chance to draw from fancy, to sketch and work out one's own idea of beauty. There was no general course of training in this art.

Some there were who had natural talent, some who perhaps were fortunate in having a superficial idea of drawing, but the great majority had only the urge to express themselves in this simple manner, and perhaps never knew the talent lurking beneath their efforts. Many, no doubt, who had the ability to choose and blend colors, lacked the faculty of drawing. But they were not hindered in their purpose, for there was always someone in the family or neighborhood who had the "knack."

And so these pioneers—these women with no precedent to follow, with little knowledge or skill in designing, planned and hooked these future heirlooms.

Truly shape and fashion these;
  Leave no yawning gaps between;
Think not, because no man sees,
  Such things will remain unseen.

In the elder days of Art
Builders wrought with greatest care
Each minute and unseen part;
For the gods see everywhere.
HENRY WADSWORTH LONGFELLOW

I would like to pay a tribute to these pioneer women! Think of their handicaps! They had to stand or bend over frames usually stretched between four chairs. If they used linen for a foundation, they had already prepared the flax through twenty dexterous manipulations, spun the thread and woven the material on a hand-loom. If their foundation was burlap, it was made of sugar or meal bags, which had first been washed, stretched and pieced together. Their hooks were forged from old metal or a nail, and success depended upon the patience and skill of the "man of the house." Their woolen materials came first from the sheep's back. But *en route* they had to first outlive a long life of usefulness as clothing or covering before New England thrift would permit them to be cut up for rugs. The material for their dyes had to be gathered from the woods, boiled and mixed, and unless they were clever in this art, they were restricted in their colors.

But after they had gathered all these things together, they still lacked their design, and for many this was the real stumbling block.

So the really fine rugs which have come to us from that period are the product of industrious and artistic women, most of them untrained, who worked out their own ideas of beauty, in color and design.

As we look at these heirlooms of the past we cannot help but wonder about the personalities of their creators. For here indeed in color and design, is the expression of the individual.

Good judgment and executive ability are proven in a well arranged and well spaced design. Industry is shown by the wide range of colors, which must have required countless hours over the dye pots. Patience is denoted by fine details. Artistic ability is apparent in the rich blending of colors. Perseverance and ambition are recognized in the size. Not all rugs have all these attributes, but most of them are outstanding in one or more of these characteristics.

These women, who lived before schools of art and design were founded, might have become artists and designers, but they lived in an age when domestic life was the rule, and their natural talent, needing some outlet, found it in the lowly frame of the hooked rug.

Most of us to-day feel a desire to do some sort of creative work, not merely so that it may be admired by friends, but for the personal gratification we get from accomplishment, and I presume the women of that period were no different. Even when the result is not satisfying, we look beneath the lines and threads and derive a certain joy from the struggles and efforts and the difficulties which were overcome. In looking at the finished product we are reminded of our thoughts as we worked—our dreams, hopes, and fears which seemed to be woven into the very warp.

Did you ever come across a bit of old embroidery which awakened memories of the dreams of the days in which it was made? I have one bit that I am still using after twenty-two years, washed and re-washed, yet neither laundry nor time can erase the flood of thoughts woven into every mesh. Every time I look at it, I recall those winter evenings during which I made it, and of my thoughts as I carefully pulled in the stitches. They were of a wedding, and particularly of a "going-away" dress which was to have been a soft shade of wisteria. It is still a thing of dreams, for that particular wedding never took place, nor have I realized that visionary suit of "soft wisteria."

Early American Original Designs

Love of creative art endears
Life to its possessor
And this genius did not know
That in far distant years
Appreciative folk, in pride,
His handiwork would show.

ARTHUR E. WINCHESTER

In most ways in our early American life the ultra-conservative predominated, and from this background we have inherited the simple, plain and quiet patterns so typical of those days.

Even the substantial hearth-stones were used for design, this one from the Governor Wentworth home.

WENTWORTH BRICK No. 2A

This design, as it is being hooked to-day, lifts this simple geometric pattern into an outstanding rug. Careful and artistic blending or combination of colors ties up to the simple border motif which repeats the high lights of the same colors. The border motif is accentuated further by a pastel or neutral background.

The basket-weave, the block patterns and the hit and miss design, sometimes dressed up with a star, or other motif, may have been the result of having little or nothing to work with, yet, who knows, perhaps it was after all just good taste to use the simplest designs with their pine furniture and wide board floors.

Even the simple twist of the skein of yarn served their purpose, as in the New England Twist—No. 60. Aided by artistic blending and a wide range of shades, this pattern can be one of the loveliest.

Even the daring design and vivid colorings may have been a safe outlet for a restricted nature.

No. 180 is one of the best examples from the heroic patterns. Note the cleverness of the artist in reversing the figures, thus securing perfect balance and eliminating a one-way rug. One of this design which cannot help but hold your attention, and in its proper place win your admiration, has been made very much like the original rug from which it was copied. Its cabbage roses were hooked with myriad hues of gorgeous ruby reds, the leaves were shaded from a light to a deep jade green and the background was a delicate putty gray. The wide border was an oxford gray, with the dashes repeating the bright colors of the flowers and leaves.

Our imagination runs riot in deciding the source of many of these designs. Scrolls particularly were copied or influenced by the carvings on Tudor furniture, paisley shawls and even tomb stones. Paper patterns of these scrolls were cherished possessions of New England women, and

Tea Box No. 127

Star No. 48

Maltese Cross No. 154

Vermont Geometric No. 86

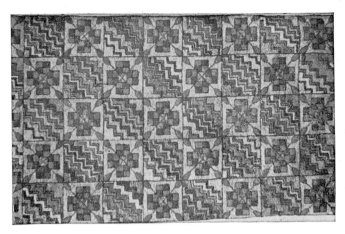

DICKSON ZIG-ZAG No. 133

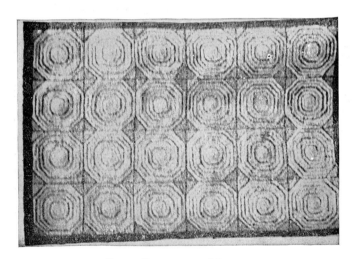

PRIZE OCTAGONAL No. 130

were loaned to neighbors, who tried to vary the designs by their own changes.

In floral centers, there was no limit to the fund of choices which they had from the old fashioned flower gardens of that time. Many of their flowers are now rare, but when the hooking and coloring have been carefully executed, one often sees flowers in these old rugs found only in the very old magazines and books.

Exact knowledge of nature, however, did not always produce the most interesting floral effects. Some of the most charming designs have many kinds of flowers growing from the central stem.

This abnormal growth of flowers used in the old designs reminds me of a very good joke on myself.

During my first winter of this work, when it was all quite new to me, I made one of my first original designs. I adapted the border from the old patterns, but the center was a brain child.

I drew upon my imagination somewhat lavishly, as I felt the pioneers had drawn upon theirs, with little thought of the normal growth of flowers.

I attended an exhibit that year for the first time as a designer. The classes then were small, and on the day of the luncheon, the pupils arrived early in the morning to spend the whole day, many of them bringing with them unfinished rugs and hooking on them during the day. Many of the pupils were strangers to me, as I was to them, and before I had been presented to them I passed among them as they hooked. Some of them were working upon the pattern of which I speak, but I was surprised to look over the shoulder of one to find that she had changed all her flowers from five to four petals. In surprise I said, "Why, you have changed all your flowers!" She replied, with great determination, "I certainly have! You never saw that type of flower with that kind of a leaf! The per-

NEW ENGLAND TWIST No. 60

HEROIC ROSE No. 180

son who designed this pattern certainly didn't know much about botany."

I learned later that she was not only a good botanist, but an art student as well!

The creator of this design had originality.

SCALLOPED SCROLL   No. 129

Note the grace and charm of the quaint spray with its many kinds of flowers growing on one stem, the sweeping scroll and feathery outlines, the clever spacing and turning of the scrolls to form the border. The original rug was found in South Paris, Maine, and is now owned by Mrs. Philip Chadbourne of Auburn, Maine. This pattern is very effective with an entire black background with feathery scrolls in many shades of delft blues and pastel flowers.

But lovelier still, to my own way of thinking, is my own rug. A taupy background for the edge, with feathery scrolls ranging from a delicate yellow to a soft dull green. Center background is a grayish white, on which the "rosy red" of the largest flower and the pastels in the smaller ones, is most effective. It is a joy to my eye every morning as I awake.

I often discover designs which I am very sure have known the hand of a man. One of these was owned by a woman almost ninety. She said that from the time she had been a small child the rug had been on her mother's floor. I think it is one of the best geometrics, and certainly one of the most intricate to copy correctly. I bow to the one who did design it!

Isn't it a beauty? It is particularly well adapted to odd sizes. One mother is now working upon a nine by twelve for the hope chest of her daughter. What a treasure for the years to come!

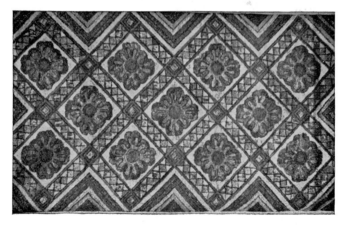

WATSON DIAMOND No. 161

Who does not love Vermont, with its low rolling hills, its intimate Green Mountains! How it must have beckoned many a farmer from other parts of New England in the earlier days! (How it still does!) No wonder that Calvin Coolidge said, with profound simplicity: "Vermont is a state I love."

Betsy Burnham Paine was born in Randolph, Vermont, in 1825. She was the daughter of one who had the spirit of the pioneer for he had set out in his ox-cart to establish a home in that State. It isn't often that we can absolutely identify one of the old rugs with its maker, but in this instance we can, for Betsy made this rug.

BACON'S FALL LEAVES—COPY No. 218

Living there amid the natural beauty of a state so rich with color, she knew and felt the urge of creation, and left her own record of this fact. With pallet and brush she had painted many a picture, and this rug was the child of her thought. From field and meadow she picked the rich autumn leaves of oak, sumac, maple, ferns, and

BACON'S FALL LEAVES—ORIGINAL RUG No. 218

others, and laid them upon her burlap, traced around them, and then copied them in all their natural beauty.

But what of the gloxinia in the corners? Was it that she wished to record the relationship between the tamed and cultured houseplant to the wild growth of nature, or was it because, as I surmise, that she was depending upon an old bluish-gray civil war uniform for her background and there must also be a relationship or a tie-up in the colors within her border. What better co-ordination than to choose her begonia leaf and blue gloxinia blossom to bind the two? It is interesting to compare the old rug with the copy. Sometimes little changes seem necessary, straightening of lines, and in this instance I rather regretfully omitted the gloxinia because it restricted the use of colors. Was it a mistake? I sometimes think so.

A quaint motif is seen in Nantucket Scrollings. Was it conceived from crumpled seaweed—the wavy lines indicating water? Or perhaps the lines left upon the sands from lapping waves? No. 74

No. 260 was called the "Inch pattern" by some, and by others, the "Boston Sidewalk"—each hooker vying with the other in using the same pattern and arriving at an entirely different design from the tiny blocks. It was not considered good taste to copy the design of your neighbor.

No. 261 is a copy of a rug designed and made by Mrs. Betsy Westgate of Claremont, New Hampshire, about one hundred years ago. The original is now owned by Mrs. R. H. Hull, of Acworth, New Hampshire.

No. 87 is one of the best of the old designs. It has balance and good proportion. The scrolls are exceptionally graceful and feathery. The flower groups at opposite corners make the design quite individual. There is nothing more typical of the old rugs than the light centers, and this one has been carefully shaded toward a very light center.

Another example of original scrolls is the Chilcott Ame-

NANTUCKET SCROLLINGS SQUARE   No. 96

NANTUCKET SCROLLINGS   No. 74

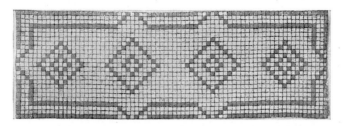

BOSTON SIDEWALK No. 260

HULL CENTURY No. 261

thyst. How they must have vied with each other to get new effects, while still clinging to the old ideas. I have a notion that the woman who made this design had a lot of fun making her queer little scrolls quite at random, yet showing a certain reserve in the design as a whole. Note the dark scroll against the light background, and the light lines of the scroll against the dark background. The young lady who made this rug (and, by the way, it was her first one), secured a subtle effect by using lighter and rather fading colors at the extremities of her floral center. No. 179

The hooker of No. 341 apparently desired to be different. I am sure she was one who could not bear to follow the masses. Her border is many shades from a full crimson red to a soft pink. The background of her floral band, a delicate gray. The floral band is in dusky pink, rose red, gold, fuchsia, and delphinium blue. This is the first time I have found dahlias (the center flowers) and fuchsias, so well hooked in the old rug that there was no mistaking them.

The border of No. 81 was taken from a museum rug. The original must have been a life's work for this was only a part of the border.

As pictured here, the background of the border is of darkest browns, the scroll made entirely of paisley shawls, the center background a delicate greenish-gray and the flowers shaded in coppers, yellows, and bronze.

Toil and be glad! Industry inspire
Into your quickened limbs her buoyant breath.
JAMES THOMSON

As in all art, there are those who stress detail and perfection. Their work may lack originality, but minute details are carefully noted and colors painstakingly blended.

BELMONT SCROLL   No. 87

CHILCOTT AMETHYST   No. 179

DAHLIAS No. 341

FARNSWORTH SCROLL No. 81

One can almost visualize these hookers. They were women who expressed these same characteristics by particular care in choosing the furnishings of their homes, they were acutely conscious of harmony in colors. They recognized balance and proper spacing. They excelled in whatever they did. They were dignified, yet could graciously bend to the demand of the moment. They were methodical in accounts, fair and square in all their dealings.

This love of detail and perfection in workmanship found a ready outlet in old designs. These characteristics are visible in many of the following designs.

Was this a nosegay copied by some clever woman from an old English wall paper? We can only guess, but certainly its originator was industrious and persevering, enjoying detail. Hooked with its flowers on a delicate tinted motif against a very dark background, it has the appearance of a cameo. I call this the "Little Gem." Isn't it well named? No. 13

No. 77B is a rug of generous proportions, and large full flowers. I can only imagine it gracing a large guest chamber beside a tall four poster. The flower looks more like a magnolia than any other flower. I wonder if it didn't originate near the Mason and Dixon line.

No. 199 is a tiny rug, only 21½ by 38½ inches.

The finest piece of workmanship I have ever seen was in this design, the hooker using twenty-two shades of red in the width of the scroll which is about two inches. The red scroll shaded lighter toward the center. It was set off by a black background, and the pastel flowers with dull cedar green leaves were lovely against an ivory background.

I call No. 111 the Murray Diamond.

Its maker must have been rather precise, yet, who knows but what friend husband took an interest in its design. It

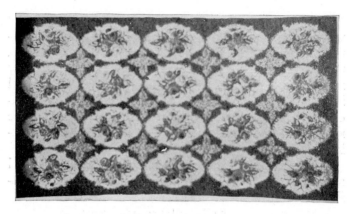

LITTLE GEM No. 13

FLORAL No. 77B

CHILCOTT SWIRL No. 199

MURRAY DIAMOND No. 111

seems to have the ear marks of a man's methodical mind.

Perhaps in no other age was there quite so much stress laid on dignity, and surely there is much evidence of this fact in the old hooked rugs. In the rugs which follow, the maker may have had imagination, artistry, perception of color, skill in accentuation,—but above any one or all of these attributes, stands dignity, the quality to which all other instincts are subservient.

No. 255 is a fine grouping of various types of design. Here we have the tiny leaf-like border, the reversed scrolls, the floral band and the bouquet center. This design is a delight to the eye when made of a brilliant peacock blue background around the outside with delicate pinks and grays in the leaf-like border. The scrolls were a pokeberry, the background within, an old ivory. The floral band and center repeated the soft pinks from the border.

Where did women get such quaint scrolls as in No. 73? Were they the feeble attempt of someone to draw something better, which in their very failure created a type of design particularly adapted for hooking?

One often sees No. 114 in the advertisements in *"Antiques Magazine."*

There is a certain freedom and abandon to the scroll which may have been the expression of one who needed an outlet. Perhaps by the time the center was reached she had regained her dignity and compromised with the traditional floral center.

Charm and dignity distinguish No. 116 as a masterpiece.

Note the apparent lack of balance in the leaves around the center, which must be treated carefully in hooking to adjust this balance by color. The background is like a painting, running from a delicate pearl gray around the floral center to a dark oxford gray in the border. Rusts and soft greens and burnished gold and copper shades in flowers and scrolls.

SMITH BUTTERFLY   No. 255

FULL CLUSTER SCROLL   No. 73

Win's Scroll   No. 114

Wing Scroll   No. 116

The creator of Eastland No. 113 may have lacked the ability to draw scrolls or flowers, but she secured a certain artistry in the undulated lines by the use of color.

Whatever may be lacking in the intricacy of design, this can still be an outstanding rug if properly treated in color. The original rug had faded into soft shades of corn yellow, light leafy greens, and dull wood browns. The high note of color, which accentuated the outlines of the diamonds in the center and border, and repeated in some of the waving lines, was a lovely sumac red. Yet I saw one even lovelier, made in the present day, in rich dark hues of copper, bronze, and green, with the main outline of old paisley, and the colors were so soft and dull that it had all the appearance of having been fashioned many years ago.

Round rugs are in the minority, perhaps because they do not fit into spaces as well as rectangulars and squares. But every one loves No. 34 when they see it. It has been made in countless combinations of color. It has the appearance of an old Dresden plate, for which it was named.

Yet from all these old designs, No. 39 is the one which Webster's Dictionary has chosen as the best example of an authentic New England hooked rug.

Many of the originals were never copied, but of course there were exceptions. Lily Beauty, No. 67B, for instance, was drawn with pencil upon old homespun, and was found in the bottom of an old trunk. It was apparently admired and copied by neighbors and friends until it had a general circulation, for I have found the design many times among antique rugs. I saw one which was priced at $275, and there is now one of this design in the Metropolitan Museum of Art. The design does not possess the ear marks of the later, well-balanced, commercial patterns. The center motif, for instance, lacks balance, yet this lack of balance is one of its charms.

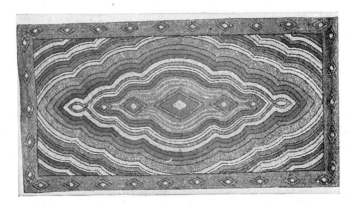

EASTLAND   No. 113

DRESDEN PLATE   No. 34

LILY BEAUTY No. 67B

But when these rugs were copied, some changes and additions were made at each hooking. Scrolls drawn off on heavy paper were duplicated and passed among neighbors, but creative ingenuity would have its way. The variety grew—the effects to be secured constantly changing. In whatever locality had the most artistic talent there one would find the finest and best rugs being made. Those made in the vicinity of Waldeboro, Maine, have acquired a reputation with the years for being ultra-artistic and exceptionally well hooked. There is the evidence of the artistry of a few, and perhaps only one woman.

> *Accomplished? She says not; but who can tell?*
> *She does some simple things, and does them well.*
> ELAINE GOODALE EASTMAN

They could not know the years of service which these rugs were going to give, because there was no precedent, nor could they foresee with what regard we would view their handicraft a century later. But if they had such thoughts, some of these specimens could not have been better done. Or was it the natural expression of those who, in doing anything, do it meticulously well?

Celebrities

AN OLD HOOKED RUG

I gaze upon an old hooked rug
Three generations sealing,
Mosaiced with bits of colored stuff
That give an eerie feeling.

I know one pattern near the edge
Was cut from Grandma's satin rare
The brown stuff patterned like a wedge
Was Uncle John's first little pair.

That bit of scarlet on the right
Was Grandpa's very gayest tie,
And when he wore it he would say,
"Inside this makes me feel knee high."

And poor Great Grandma's special dress
Made by a famous Paris house
In little patterns here and there
Run in and out like a grey mouse.

You know it really seems to me
We ought to tread with care;
Perhaps we ought, I wonder now,
Kneel on it with a prayer.

Constance Kemper

But from all this originality and imagination, from all these intricate, dignified, and conservative designs, as the case may be, there are certain rugs which stand out in my memory, as celebrities.

Aunt Harriet Fall Emery was the creator of another antique. As Harriet Fall, she lived in Lebanon, Maine, and was a most accomplished and refined young lady. It was fitting and proper that William Emery, a promising young lawyer who came to Lebanon to practice law, should fall madly in love with Harriet and marry her. She had a passion for flowers, and spent countless hours planting and tending to her beloved charges. Having unlimited ambition, she was inspired one day to create a large room-sized rug, one larger than any made by her neighbors. When the family saw the usual signs of another of her inspirations, they knew it was of no use to protest.

All summer long she gazed spell-bound at her beds of hearts ease, roses, and peonies, as if she had never seen them before, for in her mind she was conceiving a design which would include all the flowers of her beloved garden.

Then the family noticed her making frequent trips to the woods, bringing back baskets of plants, barks, and lichens, which she made into dyes. Later the lines and picket fence were covered with gayly dyed rags which hung for days to soften with the sun and the rain.

She had already spent many hours in the attic, ransacking trunks and drawers and sorting over worn clothing, but it wasn't until Fall that the family realized that this new inspiration of Harriet's was intimately to affect them all. Their usual winter clothing was missing. When sister Elizabeth went looking for her plum colored basque it was gone. Harriet replied, "Why, yes, of course I gave the attic a good cleaning of old things which have just been collecting moths, and besides," she added, "you are too old to wear such colors anyway."

But when William Emery was preparing for the Cornish Fair and couldn't find his butternut pants, then there was an argument. "Now, William," she said, "just calm down and I'll tell you what I did with them, and I guess when you see my lovely rug you'll be glad you contributed those old pants. And now that you speak of it, there is something else I want you to contribute,—I want you to make me a very large frame and get me a lot of grain bags for my foundation."

And so by Fall Aunt Harriet was in the midst of her boxes and baskets, all filled to overflowing with her hand-dyed rags, ready to make her inspiration a reality. All winter long, while the wind was howling outside, flowers began to blossom from the memory of the summer's garden. Under her skillful hook there came into being blue morning glories and canterbury bells, purple petunias, yellow tulips, and sweet peas,—even stems of rich, ripe strawberries. Not until the following June, though, did word flash among the neighbors that Aunt Harriet's rug was finished, and all flocked in to see it.

A few years later they moved to Alfred, Maine, the county seat, so that William Emery might better conduct his legal profession, and there purchased a lovely old Colonial house,—a fitting home for this beloved rug.

At first used for their own bedroom, it was later transferred to the library. I wonder if this wasn't by suggestion of William, for he was always very proud of his clever wife, and perhaps he enjoyed having this constant reminder of the talented girl he had wooed and won.

But Time makes many changes, as we shall see, and after Harriet and William had gone, it was demoted to the kitchen, then rolled up and carried to the barn chamber, and finally thrown over the wood-pile to keep it dry. There, some animal (said to be a wood-chuck) chewed a huge hole in one side.

There came a day when one who knew its worth redeemed it, and it was sold to Samuel Holloway, a New York collector, for $2050. He repaired it at a cost of $500, and re-sold it to B. Altman & Co. of New York for $4500. I talked with Mr. Haggerty of that company while in New York exhibiting, and he remembered the rug very well.

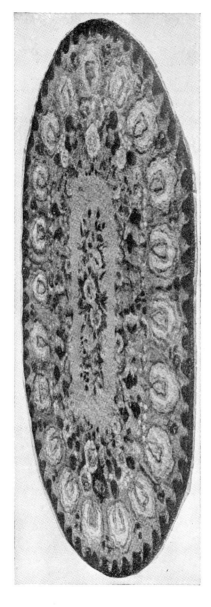

AUNT HARRIET'S RUG   No. 140

This rug, a copy of Aunt Harriet's rug, took first prize in the hooked rug division at the second national rug contest sponsored by the Eastern States Exposition. It is eight feet wide and twelve feet long.

He added to its history by telling me that they had sold it to a sister of a Southern Governor (and no doubt at a good profit), who, so far as he knew, now had it in her home.

A picture of the old rug was presented to me by Mrs. Fannie Fall Meserve, of Bar Mills, Maine, a favorite niece of Aunt Harriet's, who felt such sentiment for the old rug that she had it photographed before its sale.

I copied the pattern in 1935, and adjusted it for an eight by twelve oval. (No. 140).

But wouldn't Aunt Harriet have been surprised if someone had predicted the future of her handicraft? What a pity that she could not know of the regard we have for her artistry, and of the fabulous price which it brought a century after it was made!

It has been my aim to catch the charm of the designs originated by such women as Aunt Harriet, and bring them back to the hookers of to-day.

We call No. 178 the Double Cornucopia.

Isn't it a beauty? It is an unusual conception of the horn of plenty, a design which was used in many ways in the 1800's during the period when money was coming and going very easy.

This design was chosen by a mother as the wedding gift for her daughter. Precious sentiment was hooked into the rug, by using the red shawl which once graced Grandmother's shoulders. Great Grandfather's wedding vest contributed a lovely green. A lindsey-woolsey gown, a much dilapidated but dearly beloved hand-woven bedspread, and the little rose handbag which Grandma always carried on her wrist, were all hooked in. The entire background was made of homespun blankets woven by the great-great grandmother, who had embroidered her name (Sophia Bradstreet) into one corner. The cornucopias were

CHILCOTT DOUBLE CORNUCOPIA No. 178

BANDED FLORAL No. 66

soft grayish greens, the leafy scrolls were many shades of very deep dull garnets and cedar greens. The blankets were slightly tinted to make them an oyster white.

A delightful custom was established by using the rug upon which to stand during the wedding ceremony. Who knows how many more generations may continue this tradition. And what a lovely destiny for those beloved relics of by-gone years, to be the very foundation for the plighting of future troths.

But what delighted me most about this pattern was this. When Mr. Yacobian, of Yacobian Brothers, in Boston, who are nationally known as collectors of the oldest hooked rugs, was attending the annual exhibit in 1937, he was astonished to see this rug. In all his years of experience he had never seen but one like it. We showed him the old tattered rug from which this had been copied, and we don't know whether it was the same rug which he had seen, and in its journey through life had finally ended here, or whether it really was a duplicate.

No. 66 is one of the best examples of a museum rug. Originally made for a room sized rug, but I copied it in a size about four by five and one-half feet as a more practical size for the hooker of to-day. But think of the ambition and courage of a woman a century ago tackling a rug of that size with the detail shown in this rug. The banded border required precision and care. Weeks of preparation must have gone into this pattern before the hooker was ready to start with her rags.

I like the way the shading of the background has been deftly deepened from the lighter shades around the floral center to the darkest shades in the border. If you look carefully you will find the hooker's initials and the year 1938 hooked in two corners. No one can question the age of this rug in the years to come.

These pioneers knew the joy of their creative work, a joy which no one could borrow or steal, and we owe them, as we do all of an original or creative mind, an eternal debt.

But we cannot all be original, and all old designs are not necessarily good. Some can be improved, and it has been my aim to retain and copy the best, but make improvement where I think it can be done without sacrifice, and like the Grecian relay racer of old, carry the torch on to victory.

To be imitated, they tell us, is the greatest flattery, and many there were in those days who deserved this compliment. If you have ever hooked a rug you will know the pride with which you show your handiwork. In fact you probably have an uncontrollable desire to show it to everyone who comes your way. Women I suppose were no different a century ago. We can well imagine that this natural pride was reason enough why we to-day have these splendid examples of originality, perseverance and artistry.

"Hold high the woof, dear friends, that we may see
The cunning mixture of its colors rare.
Nothing in nature purposely is fair,
Her mingled beauties never quite agree;
But here all vivid hues that garish be,
To that tint mellow which the sense will bear,
Glow, and not wound the eye that, resting there,
Lingers to feed its gentle ecstasy.
Crimson and purple and all hues of wine,
Saffron and russet, brown and sober green
Are rich the shadowy depths of blue between;
While silver threads with golden intertwine,
To catch the glimmer of a fickle sheen,—
All the long labor of some captive queen."

GEORGE SANTAYANA

Courtesy of Mrs. Beth Frost Boadway, Pasadena, Calif.

EDWARD SANDS FROST

PART 2

The First Commercial Designer

"Lives of great men all remind us
We can make our lives sublime
And departing, leave behind us
Footprints on the sands of Time."
HENRY WADSWORTH LONGFELLOW

IT WAS in the year 1868 that the commercial pattern was originated by Mr. Edward Sands Frost, of Biddeford, Maine, a tin pedlar.

Many of my readers will remember the old time "tin pedlars." They were Yankees who had a supply of everything a homemaker needed from calico to tinware. They travelled with their loads from village to village throughout New England. In those days, when it required so much time to drive to the nearest trading center, they were welcomed from house to house and their visits were much anticipated.

These pedlars became personal friends of their customers. They had time to stop and gossip along the way and bring with them the news of what was happening in the adjacent villages. Sometimes they would barter their own goods for something the homemaker had, perhaps this was the beginning of the "rag man," for Mr. Frost tells of gathering rags and old copper boilers from his customers. It all helped to provide business, and Yankees were recognized for their gift in driving a bargain.

Edward Sands Frost was a New Year's gift to his parents, being born in Lyman, Maine, in the year 1843. Ellen Whitehouse became his bride. He enlisted in Company E of the First Maine Cavalry for service in the Civil War, and was discharged from the service of the United States in February of 1863, due to poor health. He was always frail in health. In the winter of 1864-65 he was obliged to give up his work as a machinist in the Saco Water Power machine shop and his physician recommended outdoor work.

Times were hard then, as it was the close of the great Civil War, and no doubt Mr. Frost pondered for some time before he had courage to start out with a meagre supply of articles in a tin pedlar's business which he had to develop from the very first sale. During the following four years he established regular routes and gained many customers. Retiring and reserved in manner, gentle and loveable, he had the qualities which must have made and held many friendships through his business contacts.

In making his trips through the villages he saw women hooking rugs of their own designs. While some of them were beautiful, many were crude affairs. Being a good Yankee, he pondered over the dearth of good designs and finally decided to make some himself. He was very artistic and his efforts were well rewarded, for some of the best rugs from sixty to seventy years old are of his designs, and he has proved to date the outstanding commercial designer of hooked rug patterns.

We have none too many facts with which to build a background of this man's life, in so far as it pertains to his pattern business. He probably never realized that one day we would be searching far and wide for evidence of his work—or even that he had accomplished an outstanding means of bringing beauty into the lives of countless women and that Time would one day commend him in his work.

His story of that period, and of the inception of the first stencilled rug pattern, as told to one of the *Biddeford Times* reporters while visiting Biddeford in 1888, is of great interest.

"By the advice of my physician, who recommended outdoor work, I went into the tin peddling business which

I followed till the spring of 1870. During this time, by close economy, I saved my first thousand dollars, and it was the proudest day of my life, when in January, '69, after taking account of stock, I found I had invested in household goods $200. in team outfit $175. in staple goods and cash in bank $700. As the profits did not average over two dollars per day, it had required the strictest economy to support my family and save that amount. It was a hard struggle, but that is the only way a poor man can get capital to go into business with. It is easy enough to make money, if a man has money to work with.

"It was during the winter of '68 that my wife, after saving quite a quantity of colored rags that I had collected in my business as a tin peddler, decided to work them into a rug. She went to her cousin, the late Mrs. George Twombley, and had her mark out a pattern, which she did with red chalk on a piece of burlap. After my wife had the pattern properly adjusted to her quilting frame she began to hook in the rags with the instrument then used in rug making, which was a hook made of a nail or an old gimlet. After watching her work a while I noticed that she was using a very poor hook, so, being a machinist, I went to work and made the crooked hook which was used so many years afterward in the rug business, and is still in vogue to-day.

"While making the hook I would occasionally try it on the rug to see if it was all right as to size, and in this way I got interested in the rug. I had 'caught the fever' as they used to say. So every evening I worked on the rug until it was finished, and it was while thus engaged that I first conceived the idea of working up an article that is to-day about as staple as cotton cloth and sells the world over. Every lady that ever made a rug knows that it is very pleasant and bewitching work on a pretty design, but tiresome and hard on plain figures; and so it proved to me.

After working four evenings on the rug I told my wife I thought I could make a better design myself than that we were at work on, so after we finished our rug I got a piece of burlap and taking a pencil, I wrote my first design on paper and then put it on to the cloth and worked the flower and scroll already for the ground-work.

"We showed it to our neighbors and they were so well pleased with it that I got orders for some twenty or more patterns like it within three days. So you see I got myself into business right away. I put in my time evenings and stormy days sketching designs, giving only the outlines in black. There was not money enough in it to devote my whole time to the business, and as the orders came in faster than I could fill them I began, Yankee-like, to study some way to do them quicker. Then the first idea of stencilling presented itself to me.

"Did I go to Boston to get my stencils made? Oh, no, I went out into my stable where I had some old iron and some old wash boilers I had bought for their copper bottoms, took the old tin off of them and made my first stencil out of it. Where did I get the tools? Why I found them in the same place, in my stable among the old iron. I got there some old files, half flat and half round, took them to the tin shop of Cummings & West and forged my tools to cut the stencil with. I made a cutting block out of old lead and zinc.

"After fitting myself out with tools I began making small stencils of single flowers, scrolls, leaves, buds, etc., each one on a small plate; then I could with a stencil brush print in ink in plain figures much faster than I could sketch. Thus I had reduced ten hours' labor to two and a half hours. I then had the art down fine enough to allow me to fill all my orders, so I began to print patterns and put them in my peddler's cart and offer them for sale. The news of my invention of stamped rugs spread like magic, and many a time as I drove through the streets of Biddeford and Saco, a lady would appear at the door or window, swinging an apron or sun bonnet, and shouting at the top of her voice, say 'Are you the rug man? Do you carry rugs all marked out?' I at once became known as Frost, the rug man, and many Biddeford citizens still speak of me in that same way.

"My rug business increased and I soon found that I could not print fast enough; I also found it difficult to duplicate my patterns, or make two exactly alike, as many of my customers would call for a pattern just like Mrs. So and so's. Then I began to make a whole design on one plate. At first it seemed impossible, but I was willing to try, so I obtained a sheet of zinc and printed on it and cut out a design. This process I continued to follow till I had some fourteen different designs on hand, ranging from a yard long and a half a yard wide to two yards long and a yard wide. These plates gave only the outline in black and required only one impression to make a complete pattern, yet it was by far the hardest part of the whole affair to make the stencils so as to take a good impression, and I think there is not a stencil workman in this country that would consider it possible to cut so large a plate with such fine figures and take an impression from it. It required a great deal of patience, for I was just thirty days cutting the first one and when I laid it on the table the center of the plate would not touch the table by two and a half inches. As the plate of zinc lay smooth before being cut, I knew it must be the cutting that caused the trouble; I studied into the problem and learned that in cutting, the metal expanded, so I expanded the uncut portion in proportion to that which was cut and the plate then lay smooth. This I did with a hammer, and it took about two days' time.

"When the plate was finished I could print with it a

pattern in four minutes that had previously required ten hours to sketch by hand. I then thought I had my patterns about perfect, so I began to prepare them for the market. I remember well the first trip I made through Maine and a part of New Hampshire, trying to sell my goods to the dry goods trade. I failed to find a man who dared to invest a dollar in them; in fact, people did not know what they were for, and I had to give up trying for a while and go from house to house. There I found plenty of purchasers, for I found the ladies knew what the patterns were for.

"Next I began coloring the patterns by hand, as I had some call for colored goods. The question of how to print them in colors so as to sell them at a profit seemed to be the point on which the success of the whole business hung, and it took me over three months to settle it. I shall never forget the time and place it came to me, for it had become such a study that I could not sleep nights. It was in March, 1870, one morning about two o'clock. I had been thinking how I could print the bright colors in with the dark ones so as to make good clear prints. My mind was so fixed on the problem that I could not sleep, so I turned and twisted and all at once I seemed to hear a voice in my room say: 'Print your bright colors first and then the dark ones.' That settled it, and I was so excited that I could not close my eyes in sleep the rest of the night and I tell you I was glad when morning came so that I could get to town to buy stock for the plates with which to carry out my idea.

"At the end of a week I had one design made and printed in colors. It proved a success. Then I sold my tin peddling business and hired a room in the building on Main Street just above the savings bank, where I began in the month of April (1870) to print patterns in colors. I did my own work at first for four months and then I employed one man. In September I had two men in my employ, and in November I opened a salesroom in Boston through Gibbs & Warren. Then it took four men in December and ten men during the rest of the winter. Many of the business men here will remember what an excitement my business created, for there were very few men who had any faith in my bonanza. I remember having seen well known business men stand in the street near Shaw's block and point over at my goods that were hung out and laugh at the idea (as they afterward told me) of my making a living out of such an undertaking. Well, I guess they will all admit that I did make a living out of it, as I continued to manufacture rug patterns there, all of my own designs, till the fall of '76, when I was so reduced in health that I sold out my business and left Biddeford November 2nd, for Pasadena, California, where I have since made my home."

His work was recognized with a Medal of Excellence from the American Institute Fair of New York, and a diploma from the Mechanic Fair in Boston, in the year 1878.

He sold his business to Mr. James A. Strout in 1876, and was so reduced in health that he was carried to California on a stretcher.

Regaining his health in California, he became the founder of the largest G.A.R. Post there—the J. E. Godfrey Post No. 93. Although he visited Biddeford frequently, he made his home in California until he died in May of 1894.

And so these Frost patterns have become known and recognized as the outstanding rug designs of the early commercial patterns. There are certain ear-marks of his work which can at once be recognized. These patterns, some of them having been laid away by those who purchased more than they could hook, or who lost interest in their work, are still to be found in old attics and bureau drawers, and can sometimes be picked up at auctions or antique shops.

Great was my joy when I found my first Frost burlap, in the home of Mrs. E. E. White, of Belmont, Vermont. Here was his name stencilled on the end; "E. S. Frost & Co., Biddeford, Maine." (No. 134).

With painstaking care every line was reproduced so that no detail would be omitted or accentuated. It is a delight to uncover this oriental rug in antique shops or homes, and see the many varieties of color in which it was developed years ago. The predominating colors, however, seem to be the rich reds and blues, which may have been due to an attempt to copy the real orientals, or the necessity of using the prevailing dye of indigo blue and the proverbial "red flannels" of that period.

Mr. Frost says, "I found it difficult to duplicate my patterns or make two exactly alike" during his first years of experience, and this probably accounts for the fact that I have often found two patterns apparently alike, yet differing in some slight way by the omission of buds, flowers or corner motifs. It also accounts for the fact that I first found only the center of the Maine Scroll made as an oval rug, without any scroll border.

Before I discovered the pattern as shown in illustration No. 75, I visited Vermont in my search for old designs, and there in Castleton found what I considered one of the loveliest old rugs I have ever seen, of this design. The scroll was blended from a deep rose red to a delicate shell pink. The background of the center was old ivory, the buds in the wreath a lovely old blue and the floral center was in pastels with light pinks and rose predominating. I dreamed about it for weeks after my return, and regretted that my purse had not permitted its acquisition. I was somewhat consoled however, when the same design came to me later in a rug which had been used for marriage ceremonies for three generations in a home in Maine, and I chose this pattern for the first rug I had made for my

Frost Oriental No. 134

Maine Scroll No. 75

home. The colors of my adorable rug of Castleton, Vermont, were repeated as near as memory would permit.

No. 118 is another example of one of Frost's designs which were not always reproduced the same. I have seen it sometimes with buds in the center floral motif, sometimes without. The pattern is also often seen with an endless chain for the border (as shown in this illustration), which was used for design in many ways to commemorate the laying of the cable across the Atlantic. Note the abnormal growth of flowers? This is typical of many of his designs.

But particularly so in No. 214.

While this is similar to 118, he brings a new note by using a twisted ribbon or leaf around the floral center. While his design appears to be a leaf, many hookers apparently changed it to a ribbon when hooking it.

No. 217 came to me in the form of a highly colored stencilled pattern about which Frost has written. No wonder it would take thirty days to cut the stencil of such an intricate pattern as this. If the hooker was bored with this design, it certainly wasn't Mr. Frost's fault.

No. 244 is one of his most adorable small patterns which I uncovered near Manchester, New Hampshire, where I was visiting. When I began to talk about my hobby, my friend said: "Why, I believe I have two of those stamped patterns, which belonged to my aunt. I always thought some day I would hook them, but have never got around to it." I finally made her realize that we seldom do those things which "we always intend to do sometime when we have time" and persuaded her to sell them to me, for no one would ever treasure them more than I. Used for twin rugs, this pattern was chosen as a wedding gift for my new daughter. The background is subtly mottled with many shades of delicate beige. A little "button hole" edge is hooked with a deeper shade. The charm of the design is

ENDLESS CHAIN   No. 118

GILL ANTIQUE   No. 214

brought out in the cleverly blended, alternating locked leaf scrolls, shading from yellow to old gold, and from light to dark brown. The old gold roses and turquoise leaves are surrounded by buds and small flowers which are so delicately colored they fade out into the background.

Frost made many oriental or "turkish" patterns, but No. 230 is one of the best of the smaller ones.

As one of my townswomen made the old rug which is No. 169, it has a particular appeal for me. She was a minister's wife and was known as "Madame Parker" and the rug is still in the possession of her family.

No. 46 is probably one of Mr. Frost's best known patterns. It is quite different from the others, and it would be interesting to know what inspired this unusual and rather intricate scroll border.

From a careful study of his many designs, it is my belief that his best work was accomplished at the beginning of his venture. His earliest number (1) of which he said, "I got orders for some twenty or more patterns within three days," is outstanding among all the others, and is typical of his best work which followed.

It is rather interesting to note among the papers still in the possession of his family, a letter from his sister Sarah, written on stationery headed:

OFFICE AND SALESROOM OF THE

TURKISH RUG PATTERN COMPANY

339 SIXTH AVE., NEW YORK

Patterns and materials for "Home made Turkish Rugs."

It was dated September 1, 1879, but related only to personal family affairs. This might account in some way for the oriental influence in some of his patterns. Or, having

WHITE FROST No. 217

LOCKED LEAF No. 244

LITTLE FROST ORIENTAL   No. 230

SHELDON ANTIQUE   No. 169

sold his rug business in Biddeford, Maine, in 1876, did his sister Sarah specialize on his oriental patterns in New York subsequent thereto? As his family can throw no light on this matter, we can only wonder!

Whenever one makes a success in any business there are always others to imitate or follow, and during the next few years four other commercial designers came into the market.

The *Biddeford Times,* in 1888, refers to "five establishments that manufacture that class of goods (stencilled designs), three of which were doing business in Biddeford." Mr. James A. Strout, who continued to do business under the name of E. S. Frost & Co. until 1900, was one. H. Pond was another, and the third I believe to be one named Ayers. The two outside of Maine were E. Ross & Co. of Toledo, Ohio, and Mr. John E. Garrett, of Burlington, Vermont.

I have never found but two patterns which I could identify as "Ponds" and I have never found any of Ayers.

A book of rug patterns published by E. Ross & Co. of Toledo, Ohio, is dated 1891. Mr. Ebenezer Ross and Mr. Joseph L. Parks formed the partnership known as E. Ross & Co. in Toledo, Ohio; Mr. Ross was an inventor of many things, and perfected and patented a needle which was the first "punch hook" to be used with yarn which he also sold. It is my impression that the hook and yarn were important factors in his business and the stencilled patterns were included in his catalog as a means of increasing the sale of hooks and yarn.

Most of the patterns shown were copied from Frost, and little originality is shown in the others, except by the use of animals as the center motif of the design. Not only the familiar dog, cat and kittens, but the hen with her brood of chickens, ducks, birds, lions, horses, deer, lambs and cows dominate the designs. The Odd Fellows links and the Masonic emblem are also featured. His borders feature the geometric designs and he uses leaves profusely for both borders and corners.

Mr. Garrett used leaves to a great extent and his designs are decidedly conventional and rather set. The rug shown on page 27 (no. 27) of W. W. Kent's book (*The Hooked Rug*) is one of Garrett's design.

TUDOR SCROLL No. 46

PART 3

The Creative Work of To-day

ITH the beginning of the machine age, when mass production was the "watch word" of the day, this handicraft suffered from neglect, and interest in it dwindled to a point where the patterns practically disappeared from the market, or deteriorated to the mediocre. Think of it! Within thirty years of the time when Frost declared that the stencilled hooked rug pattern "was known the world over and was as staple as cotton goods." Yet that is the case, and for many years this handicraft seemed to be forgotten. During that time women who did hook, drew their own patterns, or wasted their time on atrocious commercial designs which grew worse and cheaper.

It is only within the last fifteen or twenty years that the Early American originals, and the earliest commercial designs have come within the class of antiques, and finally inherited the respect and admiration of a new generation. These old rugs were sought by dealers and collectors alike, until now it is well nigh impossible to find a good authentic specimen on the market.

Modern machinery had made possible the imitation of these treasures, but never their reproduction, for there is no substitute for the human hand nor for painstaking and loving care. The machine-made rug served the purpose of utility, but where there was comfort and warmth for the floor there was none for the soul. No sentiment or charm was attached to make them grow dearer each year. No, there was not even memory of the nimble fingers that had chosen to spend leisure time in the fashioning of something in which there was personality.

The prices at which some of these old rugs sold is of considerable interest. The story of one such rug was told to me by an antique dealer in Dover-Foxcroft, Maine. He said a friend in a neighboring village was breaking up her home at the age of eighty. He remembered that she had a large hooked rug which her mother had made. When he heard the news he wasted no time, but immediately drove to her home some thirty miles away, arriving late in the evening. She was much amused that he had come so far at that time of the night to discuss her old hooked rug. She said, "Of course I still have it, I just rolled it up in a piece of burlap so the junkman could take it away to-morrow. But I wouldn't think of *selling* it, it isn't worth a penny, its plumb full of holes!" But to him this was a business affair, and he insisted that he pay for it. "Well," she replied, "all right then, you may buy it, if you insist. Give me a dollar and I will put it in the missionary box." However, he knew his market far better than she, and while he hadn't the slightest idea what it would really sell for, he finally succeeded in making her accept $60. for it, which seemed to her an outlandish amount. He had the rug cleansed and repaired, and the next time the New York collector came through, with very little dickering, sold it for $800. He learned later it had been re-sold for more than twice that amount.

While to-day's rugs have not the commercial value of those which have accumulated value with the years,—yet they are being recognized by those who appreciate true craftsmanship.

One instance was a map of Bermuda, hooked by Mrs. Starr of Littleton, Massachusetts, who had lived most of her life on the island.

The border was made up of various brightly colored tropical fish with coral and sea weed, and the four corners denoted the countries historically connected with the island. It was very well done, and so successful was she in reproducing the chalky white of the islands, and the gorgeous blues of the Bermuda waters, that all her friends in Bermuda greatly admired and coveted it. Among them was Mrs. James J. Storrow, of Boston, who had a home in Bermuda and desired it for that home. When she offered $300 for it Mrs. Starr could not resist.

There is much in the years which intervene between the antique period and the present day, which should be saved for other generations. There is much in the creative work of to-day which will survive and be enjoyed by our great grandchildren.

I haven't any grandchildren yet, but I already have something which I am guarding and carefully saving for them. It is a package containing a design of a room sized rug, a sample of wall paper and this story:

About 1920, Mrs. Louis Hills of Westbrook, Maine, was redecorating her living room in an old Colonial mansion. There was an old wardrobe which had been built against one end of the room. She decided to have it torn away from the wall, and when that was done she found three strips of very old fashioned wall paper in perfect condition. She appreciated its age, and carefully removing it, carried it to her decorator, Mr. Richard F. DeNeill, of Porteous, Mitchell & Braun, in Portland, who happened to have a hobby of old wall papers. He was unable to identify its age, or find its duplicate, and finally, still unidentified, placed it in the files of the Birge Manufacturing Company, specialists in historical papers.

About ten years later, Mount Vernon was being restored for the Bi-Centennial celebration of George Washington's birthday. It was discovered from bits of falling plaster that there had been wall paper beneath it.

History shows that in 1775 George Washington erected an addition to Mount Vernon. He was called away suddenly to war, before the final coat of plaster had been applied to the bedroom which he was later to occupy. Now

it seems that Martha, becoming impatient with the unfinished room, had a wall paper applied to brighten the
unfinished room. In 1802 when Bushrod Washington became the owner, the paper was covered with the final
thin coat of white plaster.

These bits of falling plaster were pieced together, but
the design was not only incomplete,—the action of the
lime had destroyed all the original coloring.

Then began a nation-wide search by the Mt. Vernon
Association, which ended in the Birge files. There was
the old paper in all its native coloring, the very sample
which Mrs. Hills had found on her walls. Immediately
plans were made to copy the almost priceless paper. The
paper was hand tinted, and the wood block from which the
paper was made was presented to the Mt. Vernon Association. The paper now covers the walls of Washington's
bedroom, and Mrs. Hills' living room in which it was
found. This is the sample which was later presented to me
by Mrs. Hills.

In 1933, Mrs. A. T. Saunders, a teacher, was lecturing in
Westbrook. After the lecture Mrs. Hills asked her to make
two seven-by-twelve-foot rugs to be designed from this
paper.

Now that was a strange order. She said to Mrs. Saunders:
"I have heard your lecture, I have seen your beautiful rugs.
You have seen my home, its antique furnishings, and here
is a sample of the paper. I leave it entirely to you." No
designs were submitted for approval, no samples of colors carried away. Mrs. Hills apparently had implicit faith
in the result.

It was a most interesting assignment. I used the panel
for the border. The pitcher and quiver on the two ends,
the lute and arrows in the center of the two sides, with
the garlands of flowers intervening. The harps were used
as corner motifs. The acanthus leaf was repeated four

Courtesy of Birge Mfg. Co.

GEORGE WASHINGTON'S WALL PAPER

times to form a border for the floral center in which the little flowers in the border were repeated.

The colors were soft tans and sepia and wood browns, the flowers in pastel shades with the rose of the sunset sky predominating and the ribbons repeating the blue of the sky. The instruments were in burnished gold.

We delivered the rugs personally, and when they were unrolled upon the floor Mrs. Hills was moved to tears of joy. The rugs completed a most beautiful room. They will never be duplicated. I feel that their relation to that priceless historical wall paper is very precious.

Who knows, but some day, like Aunt Harriet's rug, they too will inherit the respect and admiration of a future generation and become heirlooms of the past.

> *Let me but do my work from day to day*
> *In field or forest, at the desk or loom*
> *In roaring market-place, or tranquil room;*
> *Let me but find it in my heart to say,*
> *When vagrant wishes beckon me astray—*
> *"This is my work; my blessing, not my doom;*
> *Of all who live, I am the one by whom*
> *This work can best be done, in the right way."*
> *Then shall I see it not too great, nor small,*
> *To suit my spirit and to prove my powers;*
> *Then shall I cheerful greet the laboring hours,*
> *And cheerful turn, when the long shadows fall*
> *At eventide, to lay and love and rest,*
> *Because I know for me my work is best.*
> HENRY VAN DYKE

When those who love to hook have felt the urge to express themselves in this fascinating handicraft, it gave me a welcome opportunity to create new designs to fit their need. Influenced of course by the past, governed by the need of the present, I have known and loved the thrill that

Wild Rose Lattice No. 20B

Mooney Pansy No. 153

FLORAL ALL-OVER   NO. 84

BOUQUET SCROLL   NO. 92

others have had in centuries past, of creating something individual.

From such urges and desires have come these designs.

No. 20B was made especially for a bedroom. It was my first original design.

A good neighbor loved pansies, and liked to hook good big ones! See No. 153.

Although originally intended for a nine by twelve foot rug, No. 84 is well adapted to smaller sizes. The floral centers of each motif vary, and the colors of the flowers are repeated in the little curlicues on the light background.

Only the scroll of No. 92 was original. This rug was awarded second prize at the second National Exhibit of hooked rugs at Eastern States Exposition, Springfield, Mass., in September, 1935. The background was a rich dark brown and the rags for the scroll had been dyed in paisley shades. One would have thought the colors had been painted in, they were so cleverly blended.

No. 94 was made for a bedroom, and designed to tie up with an old wall paper.

Staghorn (No. 98A) is my scroll, but the lovely center was adapted from a quaint old antique rug.

The husband of the hooker of No. 159 loved iris, and she believed in pleasing him.

I made No. 104 for no one in particular, yet everyone loves it.

When Mary Queen of Scots was held a prisoner in the Tower of London she spent many hours in doing fine needle-point. No. 213 is the design which she worked upon a wall hanging which still hangs in Haddon Hall. Needless to say, the thistle represented her beloved Scotland, the rose her England, and the lily of France is so light it cannot be distinguished in the photograph. But did the interlaced bands around the motifs represent the bars in her prison?

PELHAM DIAMOND No. 94

STAGHORN SCROLL No. 98A

SHERMAN IRIS No. 159

WEDGEWOOD No. 104

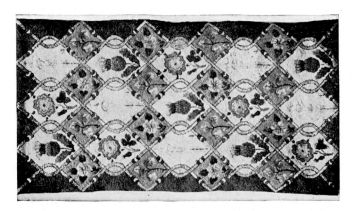

MARY QUEEN OF SCOTS No. 213

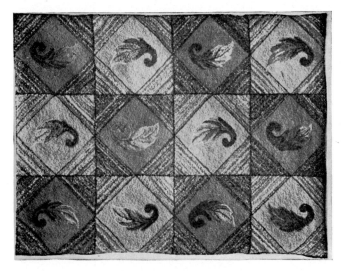

ANTIQUE LEAF No. 251

Then one day I needed something special myself. Two hall rugs. No. 251—Antique Leaf—never fails to bring words of praise. It is so livable. Many shades of light to medium browns form the background with the hit and miss corners of each square accentuating the diamond beneath the leaf. The colors in the leaves are all different. Those which are in shades of yellow to gold have many shades of lavender and purple in the veins. Those which are in deep hues of reds have many shades of yellow and orange veins. Those which are in light to dark greens have veins of light to ruby reds, yet there are no two alike.

And No. 205—Staples Runner—has a dark brown background in the border with scrolls of many shades of rich reds, running off into almost an orange at their tips. The pine cones in browns, the pine needles a light green and the fall colorings in the oak leaves make an appropriate center on a simple hit and miss background of many shades of the lighter browns.

Many of the hookers are very talented in other ways. One of them, for instance, makes pottery and tile. She had designed and made a tile table for her hall, and desired a rug which would have her own flower motif in the table repeated in a rug, and so the pattern of No. 240 was made for her.

I call No. 85 the Prize Rug. While the scroll is original, the floral center was copied from a museum rug. It was made for and first hooked by Mrs. Reuben Reed of Harvard, Massachusetts, who won the first prize at the first National Exhibit of hooked rugs at West Springfield in 1934, an exhibit in which there were more than 500 rugs entered and in which every state in the Union was represented.

The entire background was black, one side of each scroll was hooked in old faded deep blues, the other side in many soft shades of old rose and mulberry. The flowers

STAPLES RUNNER No. 205

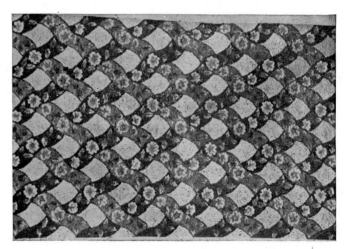

MACKAY ROSE No. 240

were in pastels. It had the appearance of feathers. The whole rug looked as though it had been made many years ago, which of course only added to its charm.

PRIZE RUG No. 85

But many color combinations have brought even the prize rug into keen competition. Scrolls of paisley on a rich dark blue background, with more definite and deeper shades in the flowers make it a most unusual rug, especially if the paisley has some intimate sentimental value. Scrolls of deep dark resplendent reds, shading as they reach the center to luscious lighter shades, upon a black background, make a beautiful border for the floral center. Its entire appearance is changed however, when its background is light,—a putty shade for instance, with scrolls of bronze and copper shades, and flowers of yellow and tea rose predominating.

STAIR RUNNERS

One of the oldest bits of evidence of patience and endurance which has been handed down to us from our industrious forebears is the stair runner. Most of them were made of simple designs, and no doubt were a means of using up the odds and ends. This may account for the prevalence of the "hit and miss" pattern. There were of course a few more pretentious patterns, but they are seldom seen to-day.

One of these is the "pictorial" stair runner. Every tread is plain or hit and miss, but the risers are pictures of houses, animals, scenery, or sometimes just floral motifs. These pictures may have had some intimate connection with the maker.

To-day our hookers are expressing themselves likewise. One of these was pictured in the *American Home Magazine* for April, 1937, and was rather unique in having a picture of the Cape Cod cottage itself on one of the risers. Another personal touch was achieved by reproducing the picket gate-way to the cottage, which included the sign over the gate "Swallows" (the name of the owner) on which two little swallows were resting.

Another one made this past winter is entirely personal. The owner is a lover of animals, and the risers are pictures of all her pets. There is her Pomeranian pup, the Great Dane, the black and white goat from the farm, her saddle pony, the muscovy duck, the turkey gobbler, the hen and her brood of chickens, the bird dogs and her husband's hunting lodge. The work has been beautifully done, the detail of every spot and mark upon each beloved pet carefully hooked in. Her husband, who at first thought she was undertaking far too much, and predicted that she would never finish it, is as proud of the result as she is, and doesn't try to hide it. And what an heirloom this is going to be for the little grandchildren who are now intimately acquainted with all these pets, and who will have this story of their play pets to bequeath to their own children. See No. 90.

There are other designs which I have made for stair runners, but to my mind, the loveliest of all is the one I chose for my own front stairs. I call it Leaves—No. 226.

The simple hit and miss center which is a combination of light beige to deep brown wood shades is bordered on each side with a garland of scroll-like leaves. They are in groups, each group having an individuality and completeness of its own, and each of these groups hooked in different colors. There is a group in shades of yellow to buff with veins of purple and orange, another in reds running from a chinese to the darkest garnet, with veins of deep green. Others of light lavender to deepest purple with veins of gold and orange, and those of various shades of green have veins of pale yellow. Usually the outside edges are in the lightest shades bringing the leaves in sharp relief against the darker background. Colorful? Yes, yet the whole has been so carefully blended, it forms a lovely border of color without being in the least riotous. Come and see it sometime when you are near my home!

And so my story ends.

Those pioneers have "left their footprints in the sands of Time." They had judgment, ability, industry, patience, perseverance, ambition, and artistic talent.

But what of our inheritance? These same characteristics to some extent are in and of us to-day. They may lie dormant,—they may occasionally stir within and make us uneasy to be "up and doing." They may haunt us in our leisure moments, and depending upon the individual, they may never really come to the surface and be expressed. And if so, what a pity!

Yet there are still many of the old pioneers—New Englanders—call them what you may,—whether living in the East, Middle or Far West, who know this urge of which I speak, and they may yet heed the call, so that they in turn will leave to others yet to come, something of their

PICTORIAL STAIR RUNNER No. 90

LEAVES No. 226

own individuality or personality for other generations to adore.

> *Rest not! Life is sweeping by*
> *Go and dare before you die;*
> *Something mighty and sublime*
> *Leave behind to conquer time!*
> *Glorious 'tis to live for aye,*
> *When these forms have passed away.*
> JOHANN WOLFGANG VON GOETHE

PART 4

A Tribute

INCE the last edition of my book, the interest in hooking rugs has grown to such an extent—and the craft itself has improved so far beyond my imagination,—that it would not be fair to issue this new edition without recognizing this growth and those who have taken part in it.

For, instead of one,—there are now hundreds of teachers conducting classes in this craft throughout the country, many of whom have associated themselves with my method of teaching and designs. Space does not permit their names—and time will of course add many more—but the name and address of the nearest teacher will be sent to any inquirer.

Each year these teachers send the best examples of their work to me, and about 300 rugs are displayed in our three day Annual Exhibits in Worcester Horticultural Hall, Worcester, Mass. Thousands of visitors travel great distances to see this inspirational Exhibit, for each year the rugs become more artistic due to the influence of good teachers.

Women with beautiful homes see in these rugs the answer to their need for appropriate floor coverings for every type of furniture from satiny pine to polished mahogany. The rugs are planned both in design and coloring to complement paper, draperies and upholstery.

Purely pleasure groups have combined their social gatherings with instruction on this worth-while "new-old" handicraft. Fingers are trained to create flowers from rags, "paint" quaint scrolls or fashion geometric designs from tiny strips of color. Husbands have been intrigued as they watch these rugs grow day by day beneath their eyes. Indeed many of them have tried their hand at it and found that "painting with rags" is just as fascinating as painting with oils.

The craft served as a wholesome escape from tragic realities during the war. Like a magic carpet the craft carried women away to another world from which they returned to routine duties refreshed. Stirred with ambition, they created rugs that brought a thrill of satisfaction in seeing their own handiwork well and beautifully done.

A century from now these rugs will have become treasured heirlooms, bearing little dates and signatures of those creating them, tucked in beneath leaf and flower.

My designs have multiplied with the years, and though they have been my hobby, they have spread out in an ever widening sphere into the homes and lives of many women. The individuality shown by them in hooking these designs will be a joy to me forever.

Many of them serve as a help and inspiration to those visiting my home, Rose Cottage (in the center of West Boylston, Mass). It is my pleasure and delight to have you visit Rose Cottage which is open to visitors during the afternoons of Monday to Friday inclusive. Do drop in!